BLACK AMERICA VS HISTORY REPEAT

Joyce Marie Lewis
Black America VS History Repeat

Published by Spines
ISBN: 979-8-89691-350-4

BLACK AMERICA VS HISTORY REPEAT

JOYCE MARIE LEWIS

CONTENTS

INTRODUCTION

The book *Black America VS The People* was published around 2013 when there was a worldwide controversy on whether the Constitution was being used for some and not others. As we took a little walk down part of Black History Lane, we discovered that the greatest speech ever written or given on freedom was delivered by Dr. Martin Luther King Jr. Therefore, the story written and the news reported were centered around his speech *"I Have A Dream,"* which is a monumental speech. Upon verbal and written report, *Black America VS The People's* case was heard in the courtroom by the Honorable Judge Randel Jefferson. A verdict of not guilty was reached after the case had been heard over a period of three days in the courtroom.

Here we are again today, after turning a few years' pages in the courtroom, to take up where we left off to resume with the issues now being more mundane. They seriously mentally and physically affect us and can't seem to be explained.

Joyce Marie Lewis

BLACK AMERICA VS HISTORY REPEAT

There are so many questions being asked, one being of what really did attack and why. There is no known host, no pure strain—something attacking out of the blue, haunting like a ghost. It came to distract us and put us at a standstill. We had to drop what we were doing, isolate, and wait for the next step to take to fight this invisible disease with initials COVID. It did invade, lurking through cities, through towns, through streets, through the whole fifty of the United States in the night and in the day, moving like a thief not wanting to get caught.

Like it's all our fault, and we summoned it from afar—this thing making us feel like all we have to look forward to is to die. Where do we put the blame, and on whom? The American people are in an uproar with questions galore of how much we can take before we break. While flights are taken, and we are ignored, how much more can our health and welfare be compromised by one coming through the White House door?

When it all ends, what will remain? The whole of the United States is wondering the same thing—what will the American people gain? Some that have occupied the Presidential Seat have done so with a colorful history. There was happiness among the people; there was some grief. Now we are under the control of an alien sitting in the Presidential Seat. Is there any ability for leadership? Is there no Presidential training, or does one come fully equipped?

Could it be possible that over the years, the Presidential Seat has been used for a cover-up or a human shield? If so, how do you think that makes the American people feel? My God. Then there was a Desert Storm. What was really going on? Helicopters lined up in a row on both sides started up at the same time, like it wouldn't cause the sand to fly and mess up the helicopter blades. Made for a non-productive day, I'd say.

Nothing would be visible until the Desert Storm cleared. The next question asked to whoever in charge near was, how do we get out of here?

Lord, we had those running as a joke, never really expecting to win. Then, when the election was won by a certain alien, America ended up wondering if she did the right thing. Becoming president was always a young boy's dream. We have to be more careful in our selecting because something said sounds good and sincere. We have to harbor that thought and enforce it come election year.

It is like having a debate between mediocre and great—who should give and who can take—while running for the Presidential Seat. America would like to know: how does one have that much power to give an unpresidential order before getting close to occupying the Presidential Seat? They wouldn't have enough juice; they wouldn't have enough heat to give out such an order that it affected the President across the border. Is one given that much authority before they even refresh the Presidential Seat? Do they have self-money rights? Where is ours? Are they self-appointed that much power? Can they get delegated that much authority in less than an hour? Is that what we're expected to believe?

Another question asked was: were we sold out to pay off a debt? We haven't gotten an answer back on that one yet. It is within my belief that America went downhill demonically. She started feeling bad; she started feeling ill. We wondered what the deal was. This happened no sooner than the Presidential Seat was filled. How are we going to recover? How are we going to heal? Above all, how are we going to rebuild?

Another question asked was: how are we going to live with this alien calling all the shots—the one that doesn't have our best interests at heart? He keeps taking us in and out, putting the media in a frenzy, no doubt. Keeping us confused, initiating violence, and adding presidential fuel to the fire while pushing all the wrong buttons. Causing us to lose our cool and do things we wouldn't normally do. Constantly playing us for fools.

Racial slurs were being made from high places. People are out of work and can't feed their babies. It's like having handouts under payments, debt following people, and they can't pay it. People are losing their homes, not having enough food to eat. Children were taken out of school. Church doors were closed, preachers sent to jail, fined for wanting to keep them open. Covenants were broken by that same token. People didn't know what to do or where to go. Idleness got old.

What about the Black History Repeat while this one occupied the Presidential Seat? It seems that we have been set back about five hundred years after being held hostage against our will. It appears there is a hidden agenda—there was one before, remember? Whoever set this unfortunate mishap in motion, it was more than just a notion. This disease appeared to be launched from across the ocean. This disease with the initials COVID—they waited until it tendered so it could take full effect on the American people. It would be easier for her to surrender and not suspect or guess, as if we didn't already have enough to deal with on our plate.

The attack was on all fifty of the United States, lying dormant, lying in wait until we'd be put under dictatorship, put in a weakened state. With their unruly tongues, what will attack us next? There is no telling. With this alien, what would be trying to bring America to her knees? Some things don't make sense and shouldn't go through the House of Senate. Some people, because of their upbringing, think that Black people don't belong here, like we don't have that right.

The time is now; the time was near; unfortunately, the time is here. The division has begun just when we thought those days were long since gone. This one needed an agent that could hit us hard, tearing our whole world apart, stabbing us in the heart. Lest we stand up together and fight for our rights, if not, America as we know it will be trumped tight.

We were hit hard with an agent that has fast-acting power —an enzyme, one that can cause sickness and death by the hour. While this one sits in his tower, trying to wipe us out, thinking he has that much clout. The COVID could be ground-up poppy seeds or some foreign flower—whatever they want us to believe. We need to hurry up and vote him out and call upon the Lord if in doubt.

Once again, the Lord will have to step in and tell old Pharaoh to "Let My People Go" and let the people know that He heard their painful cries and deliverance is on the way. This agent targets with a certain amount of radar in the field, signaling over mountains and over hills all over the world. This is really real—a grave digger is in our midst, looking for a life to steal, targeting those chronic and terminally ill.

What is its origin? Where did this disease originate from? Is it an actual virus, a bacteria, or a wheat germ? Was it released airborne? Could it have been manufactured in a lab, and the experiment went bad? The main ingredient was wrong—if so, he should have left it alone. But the agent was released on the American people once it was full-blown for some type of hostile takeover, going undetected, undercover, an enemy in disguise awaiting our demise.

While we keep reading, hearts bleeding, while the media is still in a frenzy, daily repeating, like someone is giving orders, decoding signals to blanket the American people while they are sleeping. This enemy in disguise, with a demonic plan to rid their world of red, yellow, black, off-white people of color, so to speak—all those that feel they are better than we are, and we are beneath them. They want to form some kind of WSG to get rid of the poor, the needy, the elderly, and undesirables, and only employ the wealthy.

The world won't have a place for me and you if we slip. Even though we are just pilgrims in a sojourn land, we still need to get a grip and come together. If not, we will be yoked like oxen and put in the dirt. The Taskmasters are eagerly waiting. They may even bring back the firing squad with their barbaric facade and try to get the people to turn their back on God, using different forms of brainwashing to keep us under submission, to be able to control our daily living in every phase, directly or indirectly, from a distance.

While building up a secret army for drafting or enlisting under constable tactics and conditions, we have to call upon the Lord to come save us because, when He comes, He's always right on time. We need to be in a rush because this alien has got America messed up by slithering in and attacking us with violence.

We need to unite and take the violence by force, delivering God's word. America, hold your flag up, make some noise —we have rights, we have a voice. Above all, we have a choice, but first, we've got to come together as a people and fill that void. Live, love, laugh, and be happy. Be overjoyed with the banner of Jesus Christ going before. Let them both wave. Let us get in there and start fighting to save our United States, or else all will be lost as we know it today, and too many of our people will have been sent to an early grave.

We've got to be valiant; we've got to be brave. The future of our youth is at stake. We've got scruples and morals that must be put into place. We have been set back about five thousand years—to caveman days, if you will.

As for the stimulus checks, all those buying into that—it's something to sweeten the pot before the bottom falls out. It just gives away what kind of message to the American people those that relay. You mean one man has that much power, that much clout, that he can put America in a money drought, giving orders on how the money is to be released until America gets back on her feet? The thing is, who will get the stimulus and who won't, and what do you have to do to see if you qualify, if you're eligible? Until then, we're on standby.

But there are hidden stimulus checks for the wealthy and less for the underprivileged folk. It's a joke and carries a critical aura with a film of white mist, letting us know that Satan really does exist—and has always been planning something like this—to get all the people to submit.

America has been put in a real dilemma, with even less money, and the news is always filming. What is left has to do with desperation, making people disrespectful. No one with the love of God in their heart—that's regretful. No one to direct us. People running amok in the streets, being rude, being cruel, turning into killers, rapists, thieves, and are at their wits' end trying to keep their family in food—not knowing what else to do, with nobody really to help you.

It makes you go insane. Instead, send up a little prayer to our heavenly Father to change and rearrange some things in our lives to survive.

America, which one are we going to choose? The order for us to disassemble ourselves from one another didn't come from the Lord. Stay away from each other, avoid your sister, your brother, your lovers, and significant others—husbands and wives—abstain. That wasn't in Jesus' name.

Plus, in the order, there was no howdy-howdy and never goodbye. The order didn't come from the highest on high. If we go somewhere, we have to wear a mask. Right now, it's mandatory—wear your mask all day. Stay home. Help keep each other safe.

We could be wearing the mask until hell freezes over. I wonder who will be around to finish the story—our loved ones, our friends, our babies. Again, we were asked: What else will help?

How about electing a President with a clean rep, one not full of himself, to occupy the Presidential Seat? One that has no beef.

Look at the sad condition of it all. Now I know why Jesus wept. And in dying for our sins, I know how He must have felt. His red ruby blood was shed to blanket our guilt.

America, we're being kept on a scale from one to ten. Will we win? God is watching.

Court was coming upon us fast—like in a few days—and I had to prepare my notes. There were no positive answers for this disease with the initials COVID or what caused it to graze and negatively outweigh.

There was no solid proof. It had the scientists spooked and baffled. Things were ruined the morning after when it took our livelihood, stifled our laughter. In the meantime, the Media was slamming or shutting down every statement this culprit made, pulling out Media switchblades, duplicate backup—the whole nine yards. And all he could say was, "I'm the President. What I say goes."

When were you our President? Do you really know? And if so, in name only—what was your goal? Or were you just playing a role? The American people want to know.

Look at you. Did you think you had all of the American people fooled? There are many things wrong—too many no-no's. Where do the American people fit in? What's in store for us?

Is it ashes to ashes and dust to dust? Are we under a trumped Constitution, mandated by one person, building a trumped administration for us to join? What's the point? America has already been disrespected from a Presidential Seat Elect. That means directed to me and you.

Now he wants to repeat. He has insulted the whole Black race's intelligence—like when they hung that young Black boy from a tree and left him there swinging in the breeze. Like we didn't know what that meant. They tried to cover it up by telling the family the boy committed suicide. They knew that this was a lie.

The family was devastated, heartbroken, and cried. They really brought back that part of Black History—the pain they must have felt inside.

This has to stop. This culprit can't be number one and be let loose among the people, demanding us to take a certain side. Don't let him get reborn. Let's call for the two-edged sword that the Lord spoke of and did warn. He is willing to give a demonstration to all the nations.

This culprit will be held accountable for his own actions and will be put in spiritual traction and made to apologize to the people for arousing in them the wrong kind of reactions, trying to trap them. Why doesn't he just stop running around, sneaking, always tweeting? We know that the task mastering has already begun. There should be Presidential rules about playing with the people, leading them on, and such behavior should not be excused. If you're not part of the solution, then you're part of the problem. Why push them back? Let's just solve them.

This one might have a hand in America's execution. What are we facing with the government constantly hazing, secretly plotting, planning to search and seize? We're in a state of disbelief over a possible Presidential leak—a breach of state—hiring, firing, and docking pay. The American people are stuck with needles and pins.

Question: has the back door been left open for the enemy to move in? Have we been sold out to become a Global Business? The Head of State—was he offended? A word to the wise and to the wicked: we're not that ram caught by his horns in a thicket. There are no more human sacrifices; it all ended.

There are no more surprises, Satan. It doesn't matter what you do because, in the end, you'll find this to be true—you will be through, and the joke will be on you. With God, we are going to win. Disagreeing is not an option; you are going to hit rock bottom. Look at the deck that you have stacked against us.

For the rest of our lives, we'll be stamped, maybe even chipped, not to mention altered and flipped and trumped tight. America, with this one, duck and dodge, because we're in for the fight of our lives. He feels that he has that much clout—there is no way he could be beat out of the Presidential Seat. I beg to differ. Right now, America is almost in a slump, sick and trumped.

We won't be in anything less than chains with this alien. The whole scenario we can't just disregard. We may even have shackles on our feet while Black History repeats, while he enjoys the fruits of the Presidential Seat. Our lives look grim. They were talking about the world coming to an end. There's no hope for you and me, no chance of us ever being free.

That became obsolete. Now we're just in need. God, I believe, we'll see. Whatever this one does for the American people, the facts will remain the same: it will be done begrudgingly, and the American Constitution will become a mockery.

A MISGUIDED MISSILE

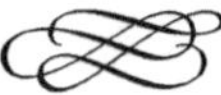

I have a lot on my mind. We have been attacked by a misguided missile that landed at a distance, sending mixed signals to hither and thither. I heard this one mumbling and saw him stumbling all over his words everywhere. It was like he was using the word 'President' as a scare tactic. Sometimes, it looked as if he was searching for something to say—an opening line. Before this one left the country, the people were just fine.

It was somewhere in early November. I had just got to town; I remember it was bitter cold. The wind was blowing snow all around, but what attacked was bitter, vicious, and colder than both of those. It was his will he wanted to impose. Did he want to see the whole fifty United States of America close and rename it Trumped Stock Hold?

Voting for him come election year, I'm deeply opposed. Just pull his stripes and say, "There's the door." Maybe he made up in his mind a long time ago to get even with all those who called him a dunce, a class clown, all talk and no show, and said he'd never amount to anything. They laughed at him. He was funny. He said, "I'll show them. I don't need the President's money; I have my own."

Every time we looked around, overseas was where he was gone—the only President I've ever known to get that much publicity. Catching the Presidential Express, staying in Presidential Suites everywhere he goes—that's a privilege that comes with occupying the Presidential Seat.

With new money, not old, there was no worry about his family not having enough to eat or running out of gas. With a Presidential pass, he didn't have to worry about how long that would last. When this one got elected, who knew he would retreat, leaving us hanging to fly overseas? And what landed with him when he came back had the initials COVID—a haunting disease.

Now America is taking you to court. You won't get an acquittal, no sir. What will your money be used for—your handshaking and messing where you shouldn't be messing? Now it's haunting you. The order should have come from you on the misguided missile experiment: abort.

On the money, it said, "In God We Trust." We will find out if there was a cloak and dagger waiting for us—a plot against the American people. In their face, we were taken back to slavery days. Where is this culprit's real place, his real home? Where does he hail from?

We're not catering while the devil gets strong with lies. Waiting, they go on and on while shape-shifting. There are no glory songs, no understanding of the people's moans and groans. Somebody needs to blow the whistle because, clearly, there is a loose cannon—a misguided missile.

Maybe when the idea was pitched overseas, where he went every chance he got, he may have thought it funny. He knew he could fund it with America's money to keep it coming. He probably thought he was very crafty and cunning and was tickled. Maybe he was being just a little fickle, trying to be the ruler, the creator, and found a way to let us know that he will censor us now, not later.

His money outweighed us. We are in for a great united fall —a misguided missile that fails to do its job and misses the mark. After it took a whole lot of planning, it took a whole lot of thought. When it's launched and takes off, in ascending, it goes out of control. It burns out the heads. The CPU seems lost until it descends and lands.

You have to discard those plans and start all over again. It could take years, but that's not one of our greatest fears—for that little project to reappear. We are not renewing the application that caused our frustration. The first one was messed up. What was low, we didn't know. He must have known it would hurt us.

When he left, we were crying out, "Impeach!" We had no idea that this one came in to deceive and wanted the America House Keys and to hold the Property Deeds. We thought that he knew what to do for the American people. We were ignored. We thought it not real—him making deals on a foreign shore, opening the door for us to be attacked by something no one can explain.

Now what's written has a different font size in directing and outlining our demise. I don't think we're completely wrong. Something shady is going on—a Trumped Stock Hold, a worldwide Barter System, a Business of his own Mr. Masterdom.

He can't get away with this if that's his intent. This one still has to account for every dollar he spent, every red cent. The color of money is not prejudiced or racist. What's going on is kind of crazed. There has to be a united change —a leap that will allow us to be sane.

In the meantime, we are supposed to be patient. Oh my Lord, goodness gracious. This one wanted to start riots, mentioning it to racist people in certain places, acting like we intruded upon their social graces. It's really disgraceful and very distasteful.

Let's talk about the Republican Party. Didn't they get sick with the COVID? Did your money speak? Did you find a secret cure? Did you get the vaccine, the antidote, and not want the American people to know?

The demonic plan you thought had no chance of failing—we hear there is no cure. This one said house products we should drink or get shot up with some kind of enzyme.

I heard that and immediately began to think that there may have been a conspiracy going and coming from across the seas. The ultimate question is: did you know that whatever is done in the dark will eventually come into the light?

Question: how peacefully do you sleep at night?

I saw this one on stage. He couldn't save face. He came to the podium and stepped to the microphone. What I heard sounded like a demonic strike to break up the American family, the American home. I immediately began to think: Satan goes back and forth, to and fro. Could this be he? If so, he seems lost and can't collect his thoughts while his foot soldiers were standing there being quiet as mice, waiting to see how he was going to get out of this or answer questions asked from the floor. Or was he going to retreat because he didn't know what to say? He couldn't think, so he went back home, which is to his fiery pit, to find something else to do wrong. All I know is that the battle is on, and to fight, we have to be spiritually and mentally strong and physically fit. We need him to stop it. We need him to quit and take his demonic crew with him. They will regret what they do working for him, the head demon, thinking we're fools. It seems kind of mental, kind of asinine. If I had a wooden nickel or a dime, I would bet that within that time, sponsored was a misguided missile. Now he doesn't know what to do. It's evident that America watches TV and decides for themselves too. Tell me, if this disease was here before, it wasn't mentioned. It didn't get this much attention. It didn't come knocking on our door or even seeping up through the floors.

When Satan makes his deals, a sickness usually follows that no man can heal. It's a fact that when we were demonically attacked, some people ended up on the street with no money, nowhere to go, with nowhere to sleep. They were put out in the cold. What's worse, it caused some to lose their faith and go astray. People were left all alone, having no place to call home. Some lost their will to live. They wanted to commit suicide, check out mentally or physically, or both. Life has already beaten them up. We are mentally drained from all the hurt, from all the suffering, all the pain. We feel empty inside, unfulfilled, unsustained. We were attacked by an unknown strain released by demonic hands. Why did this plague, this disease land? Were there others secretly shaking hands? Is he the host spreading the disease, the germ, like a ghost?

We, the American people, couldn't breathe. Now we're subject to daily search and siege. What else is in store for us while he keeps slithering and sneaking, walking back and forth, to and fro? He can be disguised as a mortal man but is a walking disaster, being cunning and crafty.

We had all of a few days to collect all of the evidence to support our plea for a verdict of guilty. We went by way of a speedy trial. The United National Victim's Circumstance Unit—this was an immediate national emergency and a call to arms by the Lord, who has his own destructive weapons. After having a discussion about the heavenly counsel, I believed that God was giving us another chance to come together as one unit and repent before all those reprobate kingdoms and disobedient nations will be coming down. They will be destroyed, and once again, the earth will be void and without form. The facts pointed out that I had to put that out there to remind us that we are in for a fight. So let's not forfeit. Let's not be afraid. Let's approach this one together, and a method we will find to slay the enemy. We are undoubtedly running out of time.

All night long, I wrote and rewrote, scribbling things out and taking notes, attacking the issues at hand, wanting justice for every woman, man, boy, and girl, everyone around the world. Whether red, yellow, black, or white, these issues we thought would never come back into our sight—now they are attacking us once again. They are threatening and need addressing.

I found that God is always right on time, listening to his people's painful cries. He doesn't make an excuse about why he couldn't come. He doesn't lie. We are walking through a wind tunnel, liking to blow our minds. The Holy Spirit pointed out to me how the American people were let down numerous times by different words, congregated smiles, and promises being rationed by the governmental pound. My fellow Americans, for a tainted crown, prestige among other material things to satisfy his demonic ego—a pipe dream for controlling and running everything, not only here, there, but everywhere. Being busier than a bee making out our criteria demonically, it's about Satan trying to bring back a dying breed to put us on a short leash in our house, messing with our mental deeds, shadowing us in the streets.

He came to disrupt and corrupt the future of our youth and distort their views and teach them how to use, while being raised in a system designed for a Black man to fail—a system of stiff-necked fools. That was a Biblical term used. God will overthrow. He will overrule.

Come on, America. We have important work to do. We have a race to run. Time is winding down. Let us raise our voices high. Come on, America, make some noise and let our heavenly Father know just how much we need him, and we will do whatever it takes to please him, and whatever it takes for Satan not to get our soul. It's about demonic counterparts in high places, playing devilish games, starring in devilish roles.

I made an itemized list of all the issues pertaining to this case, and as usual, I put it on a disc. I laid down and prayed to God before I went to sleep that tomorrow in the courtroom, we reign victorious and agree to lock and chain this alien and let God stomp him back down to the underground known as hell, where he lives, where he dwells.

The head demon, always plotting and scheming—cryptic. Keep the anti-Christ from underfoot and at a distance. So if you haven't come to Jesus Christ, you will, and invest in God and enlist in his army to pay homage so you too may live as a visionary, as a child of God. I'm sharing, loving, and caring. The intent is that I care about the people's health and welfare. I'm concerned for the souls of my fellow man and how evil lurks. It's live wires sizzling. Then people start meeting their untimely demise. Loved ones are left to pick up the pieces. The whole gist of it came as a surprise, and it was very lethal. Its mission seemed to be to take out the American people, leaving them to guess the rest.

We're stuck in a vise. There is no reason to think twice about what is going on. It's a mess, and if we don't keep up, basically, we won't get our share. It's unfair. It seems that we are governing ourselves. The seniors and elderly that can't hear or see or understand or don't have anyone to show or tell them what's what seem to be left out or trampled upon because one feels you've outlived your usefulness.

Now that you're older, people are cruel. There's no love, no compassion, only sinful actions. Helping is on the run, and as far as understanding, there is none. I'm calling upon the one and only true living God, who can make our enemies behave themselves, make them his footstool. All we have to do is believe and hope he is pleased with our daily deeds and knows that we are not just calling on him now because of our time of need. Let him know that every day we aim to serve, we aim to please, and praise his holy name daily. Repeat the same thing and get down on our knees, fall on our face, and fervently pray.

The Court

I couldn't wait for the next day to begin. I had a lot on my mind to say on behalf of the people, with the Lord speaking through me. All we can do is win, and at the end of the day, all I can say is, "Thank you, Jesus, for being my lawyer. Thank you, Lord, for being my heavenly counsel. Amen."

I tossed and turned all night, asking myself questions like: Does this mean this? Does it mean that? Did I get it right? I was crossing out lines, scribbling out words. While doing so, my patience started wearing thin. But I had to crib my notes—if they weren't right, discard, approach from a different perspective, and start all over again. Like Dr. Martin Luther King Jr., stating the facts, never rumors, even though some may have carried a little humor, I was going to defend the people with God's presence in the midst. To me, knowing that was comforting.

We planned to stop and block this demon spiritually. God is judging from His judgment seat with His grace and tender mercy, and Jesus Christ, our best friend. I have no doubt about this mystery—He will put an end to it. He did it before; He can do it again. We're in a spiritual war. I'm not trying to be clever. I'm not trying to throw my hands up and say, "Whatever." After weighing all my spiritual endeavors, Jesus Christ still reigns, and God has His hands in everything. We need not think that He doesn't know.

On my way to the courthouse at about eight-fifteen, shortly before court reconvened, I went to sit down. I looked up, and to my surprise, I saw Willie. I looked him straight in the eyes. He smiled and said, "It's been a long time. Here we are again, my friend, wondering about the same old things. We are out for justice for all—no matter red, yellow, black, or white—because the Lord created us all equal. It doesn't matter whether you're young or old, elderly or feeble; justice should be for all the people."

Then Willie said, "I'm ready. Count me in. I've done my homework too. I came to assist and support you. Together, they can call us the dynamic duo because Jesus Christ schooled us, and we know about God's measuring stick. We know spiritually when to quit. Now is not the time to frown. America, stick around—retribution is about to go down."

The next sound we heard was the bailiff saying, "All rise.

The Honorable Judge Randel Jefferson presiding. He will be hearing the case of Black America vs. History Repeat."

The bailiff continued to break it down about the responsibilities of one occupying the Presidential Seat. "You may be seated," he said.

I nudged Willie's shoulder and whispered, "This is like déjà vu."

Then we heard the judge's gavel strike and the words, "This court is now in session." Right then and there, I made a confession to God that I didn't want to leave anything to chance and nothing for guessing. I asked the Lord to give me His blessing and help me unveil, unmask a demonic frame that slithered in with no refrain.

Don't disregard—now is not the time. We should call upon the Lord, walk with Jesus Christ, and walk hard. Step by step, having faith enough to speak for ourselves. I long for a bullet-melt in my heart because it comes from God—a spiritual, warm release. The warm feeling of rejuvenation.

Don't let God catch your heart wrong. He is calling, and Jesus Christ is knocking. We have to work until His return. Don't let Him have to ask you what your heart's on. It's going to take every ounce of our faith to relate and all the strength we can muster up.

Together, we can save America and clean her up. Save us. Our heart is a good place to start—first by voicing our opinion to God in all sincerity, in all truth. God is the only one that can help me and you. We just have to do what we are supposed to do.

At any rate, as a whole people, we can't be slothful. We need to pray for strength, or else we will be too weak to take back all fifty of the United States. Alienate and eliminate all those who think they can decide our fate.

God is the Great I Am—the capital "G." Great men and women He did create, and over our lives, He does mandate. He has the last word. He is the ultimate deliverer, the judge, and is always rooting for us.

Judge Jefferson said, "I remember sitting in this very courtroom, on this very bench, oh, some years ago—quite a few. I remember you, Judy. It was the case of Black America vs. The People, concerning whether the Constitution was being used for some and not others. Here we are today, in the same courtroom, with the issue of Black America vs. History Repeat, and the people inquiring about the qualifications of one occupying the Presidential Seat—the disrespect to the American people, the lurking with a boatload of evil deeds."

The judge said, "This better be good."

I cleared my throat and guaranteed him that it would be. "You'll see," I said. Then I added, "Your Honor, may I approach the bench? There is not enough room to hold representatives from all fifty states, so I'm being the liaison to represent them. In the interest of the people, who are the key witnesses and alleged victims, we want to know at this time how the bylaws and credentials for one occupying the Presidential Seat are obtained and if they really know what occupying the Presidential Seat stands for.

"We want to know if there is a clause to uphold. Judge, the people's concerns are mine. Certain doors were closed, and idleness did get old. We have a paralegal to record, over a period of time, what transpires in the courtroom. We have a lawyer who specializes within spiritual guidelines, according to God's specific witnesses all over the world. The whole fifty states of the United States can relate and help me see the urgency of this case.

"We are in bewilderment at this time, with confusion in our minds. We'd like to take this time to prospect our findings and address what things might present themselves and put us in another predicament—another bind—bringing a bunch of sorrows and woes.

"We, the people of the United States, have the right to know, examine, and cross-examine those—and the one—who repeatedly flew back and forth overseas, to and fro, in a parallel world. This one disrespected the Presidential Seat and was allowed to repeat it.

"Another thing pointed out was the gross negligence. For as often as he went, we, the American people, want to know: In running to occupy the Presidential Seat, does one send in a résumé? What does it take today? What about one having their own agenda and daily repeating the same mistakes, still with no ability to lead but hush-hush business across the seas? I think this one thinks he's great. Nobody or nothing he appreciates unless they do his bidding for him.

"In the eyes of the American people, we have had fakes, frauds, and mysterious accomplishments in un-diverse places. Once again, thinking he's beyond reproach. No one can do whatever they want with a notion to set up a government of their own and put it into governmental motion to have a large body of people to rule.

"God is the Alpha and the Omega. We're the stiff-necked fools. God is the beginning and the end. What makes a mere man think he can just cut in and take over? When it's all said and done, God still will be the only one true living God and is with us wherever our feet may trod. No one can be in control of the elements. Scientists were trying to predict the world coming to an end, and the disease that attacked couldn't be explained. They tried to tell the people that once before. Look at what happened. What were the returns? What were the dividends?"

Your honor, as a disciple of Jesus Christ, my duty is to spiritually defend, and I'm coming to the defense of our loved ones, our kin, our brothers, significant others, our friends and fellow Americans, and those who can't defend themselves. Something conjured in foreign soil, an invisible graven image, is falling in the line of scrimmage. Satan is winning inning after inning. People started to fall out, and children were weeping. They have no one to guide them, nothing to believe in, no hope come morning, no family or friends for them in this world. It is the end.

This disease may not be a virus but something else. I keep thinking—a product taken off a bathroom shelf, one that can reinvent itself with a certain enzyme, with an ingredient that, when mixed with a less strong product, becomes crippling and attacks the immune system. It causes us to become weak and propagates through the air as we breathe. That would give this culprit free reign for his empire to activate a worldwide search and siege over states, towns, city streets, even over our domain. When this disease attacked, it probably backfired and climbed up the ladder a little higher. This one, it seemed, was out to gain our trust so he could devour us, and the Presidential Seat could help him get out of debt with the IRS—a deal offered to gain world power.

Before we get too delirious and out of sync, we must respond, react, but first think. We've got daughters; we've got sons. The youth are our future. They can't be scorned so young. They wake up, and their father and mother are gone. Whoever is running for the Presidential Seat, make sure you and this culprit don't meet. We don't need any more instant repeats. We will not stand to be used as pawns. If this one gets started with you, he won't leave you alone. Too much temptation awaits. When our children grow up and have offspring, they too will want to believe in the American dream. They can carry on and rejoice in song, praising the Lord all the day long, being straight in their dealings, being prosperous, living, loving, laughing, and being happy.

We're tired of this one handshake, making deals. We are strongly opposed to him making an appeal. We want to know—has this one ever told the truth in his life? Look at all the trouble and strife. Has he ever been for real? All in all, we have to bring this issue to The House of the Senate of State—the alleged breach, The Great Fall. How badly our bonds have been dented! That's why participating in the next election requires our utmost attention.

"I'm just not in it, okay," Judy said.

Judge Jefferson: "The case of Black America VS History Repeat will be heard by me. I heard about the mishaps that took place. I'm a little disturbed. I thought we had dissolved this issue. I'm quite perturbed."

The judge lowered his gavel once again. It made a loud knock sound. Then he said, "We will recess so you and your partner can compare notes for a quick briefing. Court will reconvene in one hour."

Willie and I walked to the park nearby. As I began talking, I began to cry. Willie asked me, "Why are you crying?" Then he asked me, "What's wrong? What's going on?"

I said, "Willie, to tell you the truth, I was really upset when the church doors were closed and the children were taken out of school. I was appalled and didn't know what to do. Just talking about it didn't help. I felt in my heart a rip, a little tear. It happened when the script was flipped, and we were attacked by an unknown agent repeatedly, silently, in the dark. Unsuspectingly, it embarked on us."

"Judy," Willie said, "you can put this to bed because we have the greatest warrior, the greatest lawyer, and judge back at the old homestead that can heal the sick and raise the dead. God is the only Head. And as God's prophet, as His anointed, no one can touch you, no one can harm you. Be God's instrument, His vessel. Let Him use you. Put on the whole armor of God and remember—it won't be you speaking but the Lord speaking through you. Jesus Christ and our Father God have your back every day. So don't worry about what to say. Just be truthful. Tell the story, not with a spin, not with thistles. Tell them about a dense-brain Misguided Missile that was launched, that was more than a hunch. Tell them about all the other issues on your list. You have a worldwide audience. America is listening. God is too. So don't ponder, don't wonder. To thy own self be true."

"Are you ready to go back into the courtroom?" Willie asked. "And lay it all on the line? Our lawyer, our counselor, Jesus Christ, never lost a case. He doesn't have to save face. Don't get ahead of yourself," said Willie. "You can keep the pace with God's amazing grace. And after it's all said and done, you can sit and relax because you spiritually presented the facts of your case. Don't forget the highlights. Get directly to the point. Always make direct eye contact. Don't ever dwell on hearsay. Over this case, God is also presiding. And as you speak, He'll be there as your translator."

People may think I'm joking, but you'll be proud that you got it off your chest. You went that extra mile of the way and did your very best. You have no reason to do anything else but smile. You gave a large body of people, who had nothing to look forward to, something to hope for today. You may have even led someone to the throne of grace, and they went running, crying, "Lord, Lord, what must I do to be saved?"

As we entered the courtroom, I took a deep breath. My heart was beating fast in my chest. I said to myself, "I'm just going to open and let God do the rest." When we got to *Black History vs. History Repeat* with a shadow of *Black History vs. The People*, there were issues to repeat. They are not just scratching the surface—the cuts are really deep. The violent, prejudiced part we thought we had left somewhere in the dark of the ancient ages still lingers, but some people's thoughts remain outrageous. They want to take that violent part of Black History off the shelf and bring it back to taunt us until there is none of us left. Satan likes to stir up trouble in high places, and it ended up being very racist.

I asked Willie to sit close by me for moral support. "I'm going to voice this for whatever it's worth. It's just me and a world full of people in fifty states in need. We seem to be a dying breed. God bless America, Lord; this is my plea. We are very sensitive. When cut, we bleed the same. We are all brothers and sisters in Jesus Christ's name. When the blood comes out, it's blue. Until the air hits it, then it turns red. We are all equal—that's what the Lord said."

We heard the judge's gavel strike again. It was time for me to get up and do some mind traveling. The judge called for opening statements. My mind had wandered off for a minute. I was in it for the long haul. For a second, it seemed so far away. Then I heard the judge say, "Miss Judy, opening statements."

I got up reluctantly and asked the Lord to strengthen me. I looked at Willie. He winked and gave me the thumbs-up sign. Suddenly, I felt a little more confident and sure that I could do this for the spiritual concerns of the people's hearts and minds that stifled it because of the dilemma we're now in. I felt myself coming back to the present time.

I began with a message to America on her Bicentennial Day, 1776–1976:

2 Chronicles 7:14

"And the Lord said, if my people are called by my name will humble themselves and pray, search for me, repent of their evil ways, then I will hear from heaven and forgive their sins and heal their country."

We, the people of the United States, don't need the type of leadership we have had in the past. We need the type of leadership today that will go above and beyond the call of duty to install peace, love, happiness, and harmony among a large body of people, regardless of race, color, or creed, and stand up to defeat the enemy while emphasizing the fact that a house divided against itself cannot and will not stand.

Conspiring with the enemy is not an option. We almost hit rock bottom considering the source where it came from. It's not easy to govern a country as vast as it is, basically by oneself, with all that needs to be done and said to keep this country great and free from previous mistakes. By keeping the people satisfied and allied, we must come together and understand why we fought to get rid of the things that cause us to have bad attitudes and negative thoughts. We have to find a way to let go of the old and bring in the new for the common good of the people.

"I'm behind you one hundred percent," said Willie, "and I'll do what I can to help support a great effort."

We must realize that time brings about change, just as faith without works is dead. I don't think that anything needs to be changed in the American Constitution—it was written for us. It just needs to be enforced to the letter and not divided with fine print or a hint of prejudice. No matter what position one holds, they shouldn't think it's changeable by whatever authority would make us vulnerable and the whole system of the government definable.

We need to bring the double standards, the hidden agendas and clauses, the under-the-table dealings, and by-laws with fine print of the system to a screeching halt. We don't need tweeters, fly-by-night overseas trips whenever one pleases, in the Presidential Jet Express, seeing the people of the United States less and less.

We, the American people, want to be able to say, "Mr. President, the American people applaud you for your good intent. Thank you for hanging in there with us. You have our utmost respect. Salute."

Before going back to my seat, I gave a little sigh of relief. I felt like I opened another door; victory was visible, the facts critical. My mind wandered off again until I heard the judge's gavel strike. I zoomed back just in time to hear him say, "Court dismissed. We will reconvene at eight fifteen tomorrow morning." Then there was a final strike of his gavel, then he retired to his chambers. As we filed out of the courtroom, I couldn't wait to get into the next phase of this, Willie, at that little coffee shop we went to last time. We talked and compared notes until they were about to close. Then we had to stop. Willie walked me home and said, "Good night, see you later," then went on his way. When I got inside and closed the door, I realized that I should have asked him to stay on the case of Black America VS History Repeat. We made an awesome team. We worked very closely, day and night, with God leading the way, with His glory light shining ever so bright that the visuals of the next court day came into my sight, along with an idea I did invite about the mystery of the Misguided Missile. The Aeronautics for Moon walking... there has been no more discussion, no more talk. We're moon walking down here in fear with masks and everything. We were hit with a disease that would come from a dense part of the brain in a demonic being from down in a dungeon with controls, like an old exotic PlayStation game, rigged with demonic instructions for destruction so he can always win. Satan does that kind of thing, blocks out goodness, and throws in temptation disguised as a good deed to shut our mouths and just look the other way, just let it happen, have nothing to say, while his followers are laughing and clapping and are trumped tight with all spades, trapping us on his own personal stage, making us tremble, making us weak, taking us back to a time where we didn't need to be. We didn't think some Black History would repeat—a time we didn't want to remember. Now, in this time, our freedom light seems to grow a little dimmer. As I looked at my notes again, I had to call Willie in. He came right away. I told him about the visualization, how I envisioned a game of Child's Play, like "Pin the Tail on the Donkey," so to speak, with this plan, this culprit could get all the way from down under and bring his business top side. The only ones that can help us now are God and His only begotten Son, Jesus Christ, to set us free and save our lives—the Holy Trinity. There is only one kingdom; God will tear all the others down. If there was a time to believe, the time is now. Who builds a tower with the numbers 666, the mark of the devil, brick by brick, layer by layer? But Satan, the soul master slayer... some people are driven by greed, material things, and jealousies that please and can get them what they want. How long will it take the American people to see that this one is just a front? He came to rob, kill, and steal our very lives, creeping, crawling around at night. Where is the best place to hide except in plain sight, looking like one of us? This alien may be the host. How best to overtake us without the gravity pull, the upside of down? Since he couldn't breathe, it was too close to heaven. Even though he looks dumbfounded, he found a way to keep us grounded from everything. Now we can't even hear the church bells ring. God is not pleased.

Michael, the Archangel, was released. He was sent down with a scroll. Written on it was a special decree, a message from the Lord for me to preach with fire and brimstone: "Stay in the Revelation until Jesus comes; you feed My flock. Your progress, don't let Satan block or stop." Tick-tock went my spiritual clock. Willie and I began to pray. Music was all around—such beautiful, angelic sounds. Their angel wings were fluttering. I saw them in a silhouette on the wall. I saw angelic faces. I was in awe, but it was clarified by God. It became clear to me how to fight this situation, how to proceed. This was a travesty, some kind of demonic plot. The whole relation is to shut down you and me, to shut down the nation. This culprit, not from this earth, Trump Alien Nation, still trying to weaken us by thought. He tried mind affixation by death termination. I don't care where he throws his fiery darts, as long as they're not aimed to hurt America's heart, the American dream. He's in it for a money scheme, it seems, and wants to destroy the homeland of milk and honey. All in all, making sure man is in ruins—that's not funny for a President; it's unbecoming. I walked in the other room and read the handwriting on the wall. The Holy Spirit called to my attention: Genesis 11: 4-8.

Verse 4 - "And they said, Go to, let us build a city and a tower whose top may reach unto heaven, and let us make us a name, lest we be scattered abroad upon the face of the earth."

The Confusion of Tongues

Verse 5 - "And the Lord came down to see the city and the tower, which the children of men built."

Verse 6 - "And the Lord said, Behold, the people are one, and they have all one language, and this they begin to do, and now nothing will be restricted from them which they have imagined to do."

Verse 7 - "Go to, let us go down, and there confound their language, that they may not understand one another's speech. So the Lord scattered them abroad from thence upon the face of the earth, and they left off to build a city."

The Bad Seed

Genesis 6:3

And the Lord said, "My spirit shall not always strive with man, for that he is flesh; yet his days shall be an hundred and twenty years."

The Hostile Takeover

Genesis 3:1-5

Verse 1: Now the serpent was more subtil than any beast of the field which the Lord God had made. And the woman said to the serpent, "We may eat of the fruit of the tree of the garden, but of the fruit of the tree which is in the midst of the garden, God hath said, 'Ye shall not eat of it, neither touch it, lest ye die.'" And the serpent said to the woman,

"Ye shall not surely die. God doth know that in the day ye eat thereof, then your eyes will be opened, and ye shall be gods, knowing good and evil."

Upon entering the courtroom to resume and take up where we left off, Willie and I thought about how we were going to reach this verdict of guilty and exactly what Trump was accused of. For one, the lack of love and interest in the people; two, he wanted to tear down and murmur, murmur, murmur about everything past Presidents accomplished before him for the health and welfare of the people. That was his goal, his plan—to put his label there. The American people were caught up in a hidden agenda; he wasn't a first-time offender. Trump literally didn't want to be nameless—how else to become immediately famous? We have to be just, we have to be fair. The American people need a President who cares, not a fly-by-night, always out of sight, for our very existence. This became obsolete when this one was put in office and didn't think he had to reap what he sowed. Neglect was clearly a fact when he kept leaving the country and making deals behind our back, trying to change the name of the motherland. How can we account for that when we continue to be governed by this alien leading us into captivity?

I made an itemized list of accusations to read to the court. It was the gross negligence, a hidden agenda, and treason to the American people of the United States—trying to go down in history for occupying the Presidential seat, but under a trumped-up empire, a tainted treaty, a hostile takeover that will render us helpless, death by sabotage. Will this alien launch the rest of the plan of attack on the Americans to take out and put in what he wants, even rename it and call it "Nation Trump"?

As a child going to school, he must have been called a dunce and told he would never amount to anything. The best way to attack us was to come through the back and leave out the front. Downsize the National Defense so they couldn't pull his calling card—patriotism. We had to blow the whistle; we were clearly attacked by a misguided missile, a scientific screw-up, an experiment gone wrong. But this one had to take it on. Maybe he didn't have all the money to pay for the antidote once he weakened America, and she started to gag and choke. Someone was lying, because almost immediately the American people started dying. Whether or not that was the intent, lots of hours and huge amounts of money were spent. Prejudiced old faithful Black people were very distasteful and put him in disgust. White people, racists, were devising a plan to get rid of us. He couldn't without putting in jeopardy his own kind. Even though this one was supposed to be impeached, he still had the authority of the Presidential seat in control of our money. The statement should be: "Cease fire. You had your turn; now it's ours. Let him go sit high in his tower and leave us alone so once again America can be strong." We found this alien to be selfish. We found him to slither with an agenda of his own, wanting to be so much the master but bigger, the creator—the Masterdom. He has no respect for anyone; he wants his own kingdom. We're tired of singing those same old sad songs with shackles on our feet. God help us this time if Black America vs. History repeats. We can barely rest now; we can hardly sleep. We're trying not to let the coldness of a calculated colored war seep.

Dr. Martin Luther King Jr. tried to right the wrongs with his speech, "I Have a Dream," and his march for freedom lingers on. We have to stay alert because of how evil lurks. The evidence was the closing of the church doors, the whole foundation of our rebirth. The spiritual songs of the Blacks, because that's all we had. Our women were raped and beaten, our families destroyed, torn apart. What we had to do was depend on the Lord and His word to fill that void, stop the pain and suffering, in Jesus' name.

NATIONAL SPIRITUAL PEP TALK

Predictions in the Bible were made starting from the old task-mastering days to the new Black America vs. History Repeats. This is our overview from the old to the new. The question asked was, what does it constitute? All the statements made concerning this itemized list are true. We were adjourned for recess for an hour. During this time, I asked Willie if he thought it would be a good idea to attach a National Spiritual Pep Talk in conclusion. Nothing elaborate or long, but straight to the point. I collected my thoughts. The time seemed to fly by, but I knew mainly what I wanted to say. In about fifteen minutes, we started filing back into the courtroom. In about five minutes, we heard, "All rise. The Honorable Judge Randel Jefferson presiding." "You may be seated." I got a little nervous as the judge asked the paralegal to read what had already transpired in the courtroom. Then he called for any closing remarks before he rendered the verdict of guilty or not guilty. I said, "Your Honor, I'd like to give a short National Spiritual Pep Talk, if I may, if time permits."

"Okay," Judy said.

Judge Jefferson, I started off by saying, "My fellow Americans, my brothers and sisters in Christ, we all have come from a mighty long way in our own way, as far as accomplishments in certain things. But we are still restricted in some other things, which puts a limitation on things and makes it next to impossible to ally ourselves to each other. We have not mastered the living-together factor to a science, but we have minimized the problems of being able to at least tolerate one another to some extent. If we can govern ourselves in a manner where our unity will strengthen us as a people, we, the house as a whole, cannot be divided. Therefore, we, together, will be able to stand because the government is for the people, of the people, and by the people. There is nothing they can do without us, and nothing we can do without each other."

There has been speech after speech of "Can we all just get along?" and "Why can't we?" Well, can we? Let go and stop trying to hold on to those things that only brought thistles and thrones into our lives because of our upbringing, because of what was instilled in children, husbands, wives, Black people being downsized, Whites stepping all over their pride. We, like you, are trying to keep America alive, help keep America great. But we have had some issues.

There have been a lot of mistakes with the House of Senate. It's too easy for one to occupy the Presidential Seat. It seems all the credentials they need to have is a little money. They did a few things but have a crooked degree; this one obtained demonically. We're all subject to change, but so-called new blood elects the same old thing—a historical shame. Nobody wants to accept change unless it's wearing their name and they have their three minutes of fame. The House is daily airing its dirty laundry from Monday to Sunday. They try to change the subject, never mentioning the attention of the American people or the United States' peace of mind, not putting their thoughts above one time.

We often feel we need a referee because Black History seems to repeat itself, and we want any part. America, please open and examine your heart. Make room to expand. Get ready to let go and let God in to change and rearrange some things. Help us see where His glory came in and lifted us up and counted us as a whole people, wrong or right. Jesus said, red, yellow, black, or white, we are all precious in His sight. We have to believe. If not, we will grieve. Some Black people are prejudiced and need to let go of some things, too. A lot of yesteryears need to be overruled. We need to come together, unite, and our youth on new history need to be schooled.

We need to talk about what is still wrong, why we feel so strongly about letting a certain part of Black History go.

Let's talk to each other more, broaden our horizons, take out the old and bring in some new beginnings for me and you. Stop making resolutions and get to the solutions. Inspire one another, be our best friends, neighbors, sisters, and brothers. Learn how to live, laugh, and be happy again. Don't bow down to the almighty dollar or to this one who thinks he's so clever and a scholar. Look to the one that loves you the most in His house, our perfect host—one that will help us and has our best interest at heart. Look to the Master of the universe, of the heavens, of the creation of everything: the Alpha, the Omega, the Almighty, the Beginning, and the End. That's the only way we can win—with God and Jesus Christ on our team. Everyone might not be for them, but those who are, they carry more than five stars; they are the whole planetarium system. Those that don't know, know: wake up! You'll be sorry you missed them both. Relay this Spiritual National Pep Talk to your family, your friends, your lovers, your significant others, all around the world. Let your love light shine—every man, woman, boy, and girl—and we'll do just fine. And together, as a whole people, we'll be more than alert next time.

January 2, 2025

Joyce Marie Lewis (Submitted)

THE VERDICT

Thank you, Judy, for that national spiritual pep talk. We need more spiritual pep talks. It seems that we've taken the pep and spirit out of the talks and made them sound like we wanted them to sound. That talk had some words in it that I really like: unity, togetherness, people as a whole. That's certainly something to think about. I went over all my notes, all examples in this itemized list. After careful deliberation, the verdict of guilty was reached unanimously on all counts. I called up to the Supreme Court with our findings for a second opinion. It was decided that there were definitely things done unbecoming of a President, and there was clearly gross negligence as far as the American people were concerned. The Black America vs. History Repeat was evident with the tree incident, etc. It screamed guilty beyond measure.

Recommendations

My recommendation is that he be referred to a psychiatric facility immediately with the statement of apathy and inability to adapt to Presidential life, with no regard for authority, and that he never be able to run in a Presidential Election again, foreign or domestic. We find in judgment for the people. The judge struck his gavel and said, "Case dismissed."

Judge Randel Jefferson (Submitted)

Willie and I walked across the street to that little coffee shop to celebrate afterward. He took me to his house. I didn't know that he lived here. I thought he just came up for the trial. We were talking and found out that we really did like each other. I felt kind of shy around him, though. He said we didn't have to rush into anything. Besides, we did a lot of research together and tackled a lot of issues. It was awesome working side by side with him. He was very gentlemanly, and I liked the way he asked me my opinion about things. I had never been with anyone I could talk to before, or who was even interested in what I had to say about anything. Basically, they didn't have time for me; they made me feel worthless, but I felt wonderful around him. We saw each other almost every day and met at our favorite cafe. We were happy and hoped that Black History won't repeat itself, and that this alien will fold up his tent and go home and not cause a cold war called World War Three.

The End

www.ingramcontent.com/pod-product-compliance
Lightning Source LLC
LaVergne TN
LVHW010506160826
845677LV00012B/2685
9798896913504